Truth the Poet Sings

Unity Books
Unity Village, Missouri

Cover photo by
Alan W. Peterson
Slice of Life Photos
Duluth, MN

Contents

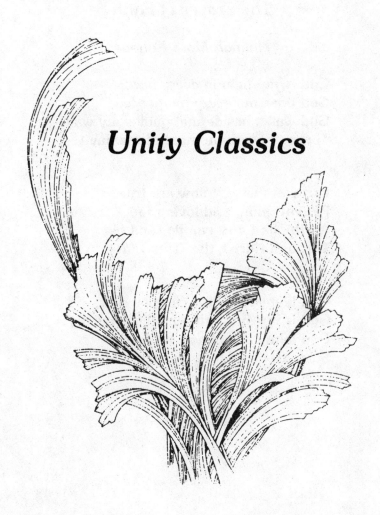

Unity Classics

The Prayer of Faith

Hannah More Kohaus

God is my help in every need;
God does my every hunger feed;
God walks beside me, guides my way
Through every moment of the day.

I now am wise, I now am true,
Patient, kind, and loving too.
All things I am, can do, and be
Through Christ, the Truth that is in me.

God is my health, I can't be sick;
God is my strength, unfailing, quick;
God is my all, I know no fear,
Since God and love and Truth are here.

Prayer for Protection

James Dillet Freeman

The light of God surrounds me;
The love of God enfolds me;
The power of God protects me;
The presence of God watches over me.
Wherever I am, God is!

The light of God surrounds you;
The love of God enfolds you;
The power of God protects you;
The presence of God watches over you.
Wherever you are, God is!

The light of God surrounds us;
The love of God enfolds us;
The power of God protects us;
The presence of God watches over us.
Wherever we are, God is!

My Love to Thee

Adapted from "The Rosary"

Myrtle Fillmore

The hours I've spent with Thee, dear Lord,
   Are pearls of priceless worth to me.
My soul, my being merge in sweet accord,
   In love for Thee, in love for Thee.

Each hour a pearl, each pearl a prayer,
   Binding Thy presence close to me;
I only know that Thou art there,
   And I am lost in Thee.

Oh, glorious joys that thrill and bless!
   Oh, visions sweet of love divine!
My soul its rapturous bliss can ill express
   That Thou art mine, O Lord! that Thou art mine!

The Answer

Lowell Fillmore

When for a purpose
I had prayed and prayed and prayed
Until my words seemed worn and bare
    With arduous use,
And I had knocked and asked and
        knocked and asked again,
And all my fervor and persistence brought no hope,
I paused to give my weary brain a rest
And ceased my anxious human cry.
    In that still moment,
After self had tried and failed,
There came a glorious vision of God's power,
And, lo, my prayer was answered in that hour.

God Knows the Answer

Frank B. Whitney

I question not God's means or ways,
Or how He uses time or days,
To answer every call or prayer;
I know He will, somehow, somewhere.

I question not the time or place
When I shall feel His love and grace;
I only know that I believe,
And richest blessings shall receive.

I cannot doubt that He'll attend
My every call, and that He'll send
A ministering angel fair,
In answer to my faithful prayer.

I Am Stronger than My Fears

Hannah More Kohaus

I am stronger than my fears,
I am wiser than my years,
I am gladder than my tears;
    For I am His image.

I am better than my deeds,
I am holier than my creeds,
I am wealthier than my needs;
    For I am His image.

He whose image thus I bear,
And whose likeness I shall share,
All His glory will declare
    Through the "I": His image.

The Traveler

James Dillet Freeman

He has put on invisibility.
Dear Lord, I cannot see—
But this I know, although the road ascends
And passes from my sight,
That there will be no night;
That You will take him gently by the hand
And lead him on
Along the road of life that never ends,
And he will find it is not death but dawn.
I do not doubt that You are there as here,
And You will hold him dear.

Our life did not begin with birth,
It is not of the earth;
And this that we call death, it is no more
Than the opening and closing of a door—
And in Your house how many rooms must be
Beyond this one where we rest momently.

Dear Lord, I thank You for the faith that frees,
The love that knows it cannot lose its own;
The love that, looking through the shadows, sees
That You and he and I are ever one!

Beginning Again

Frank B. Whitney

It matters not what may befall;
Beyond all else I hear the call
   "You can begin again."
My courage rises when I hear
God's voice allay the thought of fear
And when He whispers gently, near,
   "You can begin again."

When once quite all the world seemed wrong,
Throughout its din I heard His song,
   "You can begin again."
An inner joy within me stirred,
I treasured each assuring word,
My heart was lifted when I heard,
   "You can begin again."

Begin again? Another chance?
Can even I make an advance?
   "You can begin again."
Begin at once by taking heart
And knowing God—of you He's part!
New life to you He will impart!
   You can begin again.

This Is the Year!

Russell A. Kemp

Wonderful, wonderful, fortunate you,
This is the year that your dreams come true!
This is the year that your ships come in;
This is the year you find Christ within.
This is the year you are glad to live;
This is the year you have much to give.
This is the year when you know the Truth;
This is the year when you find new youth.
This is the year that brings happiness;
This is the year you will live to bless.
Wonderful, wonderful, fortunate you,
This is the year that your dreams come true!

The Goal

Ella Wheeler Wilcox

All roads that lead to God are good;
　　What matters it, your faith or mine;
　　Both center at the goal divine
Of love's eternal brotherhood.

A thousand creeds have come and gone;
　　But what is that to you or me?
　　Creeds are but branches of a tree,
The root of love lives on and on.

Though branch by branch proves withered wood,
　　The root is warm with precious wine;
　　Then keep your faith, and leave me mine;
All roads that lead to God are good.

A Transcendent Treatment

H. B. Jeffery

"As Moses lifted up the serpent in the wilderness, even so must the Son of man be lifted up."

Beloved of God—greeting!

In my integrity within me, where I know and see as God, I know and see you, O beloved, to be free, wise, and immortal!

I see you unfettered and unbound, triumphant! glorious! splendid!

I see you unweighted by human thought of limitation, unweighted by matter!

I see you unbound, undiseased, buoyant!

I see you strong! mighty! forceful! powerful! divine!

I see your eye lit with fire from on high!

I see your tongue tipped with celestial instructions!

I behold you bright! joyous!

I see you victorious! undaunted!

I see you spotless! beautiful!

I see you deathless, abiding!

I see you flawless! fearless! transcending yourself and all your affairs—independent!

I see you smiling! sound! sane! strong!

I see you to be the strong son of God, brother of Jesus Christ and joint heir of the Father to the kingdom!

I see you alive with God and upheld by His free Spirit forever!

All the world sees you as I see you, now and evermore.

Blessing for a Church

James Dillet Freeman

This is God's house.

May we who come here not only find out about God, but find God.

May there be beauty in this place, but especially may it be a place where men and women become aware of the beauty in themselves.

May this be a place of worship. May this be a place of instruction. May this be a place of singing. May this be a place of prayer.

But for us who worship and take instruction and sing and pray, may this always be a place of inner stillness, where we may listen and hear when God speaks.

May whoever ministers here minister in love. May whoever teaches here teach truth. May whoever serves here serve pleasantly.

May everyone come into this house in expectation and go with thanksgiving, and may anyone who comes needing help go feeling blest.

May this be such a house that Jesus Christ—or any stranger, even one of the least—would feel in it that He was with friends. Amen.

I Am There

James Dillet Freeman

Do you need Me?
I am there.
You cannot see Me, yet I am the light you see by.
You cannot hear Me, yet I speak through your voice.
You cannot feel Me, yet I am the power at work in your
    hands.
I am at work, though you do not understand My ways.
I am at work, though you do not recognize My works.
I am not strange visions. I am not mysteries.
Only in absolute stillness, beyond self, can you know Me
    as I am, and then but as a feeling and a faith.
Yet I am there. Yet I hear. Yet I answer.
When you need Me, I am there.
Even if you deny Me, I am there.
Even when you feel most alone, I am there.
Even in your fears, I am there.
Even in your pain, I am there.
I am there when you pray and when you do not pray.
I am in you, and you are in Me.

Only in your mind can you feel separate from Me, for
only in your mind are the mists of "yours" and
"mine."
Yet only with your mind can you know Me and experi-
ence Me.
Empty your heart of empty fears.
When you get yourself out of the way, I am there.
You can of yourself do nothing, but I can do all.
And I am in all.
Though you may not see the good, good is there, for
I am there.
I am there because I have to be, because I am.
Only in Me does the world have meaning; only out of Me
does the world take form; only because of Me does
the world go forward.
I am the law on which the movement of the stars and the
growth of living cells are founded.
I am the love that is the law's fulfilling. I am assurance.
I am peace. I am oneness. I am the law that you can
live by. I am the love that you can cling to. I am
your assurance. I am your peace. I am one with
you. I am.
Though you fail to find Me, I do not fail you.
Though your faith in Me is unsure, My faith in you never
wavers, because I know you, because I love you.
Beloved, I am there.

Thank You

Lowell Fillmore

A happy little thought,
Like a joyous little bird,
Flitted through my mind today
And chased a cloud of gloom away
As in and out it whirred.

No Other Way

Martha Smock

Could we but see the pattern of our days,
We should discern how devious were the ways
By which we came to this, the present time,
This place in life; and we should see the climb
Our soul has made up through the years.
We should forget the hurts, the wanderings, the fears,
The wastelands of our life, and know
That we could come no other way or grow
Into our good without these steps our feet
Found hard to take, our faith found hard to meet.
The road of life winds on, and we like travelers go
From turn to turn until we come to know
The truth that life is endless and that we
Forever are inhabitants of all eternity.

A Prayer for a House

James Dillet Freeman

Lord, bless this house—

so that any who pass by it
will be more aware of beauty—

so that any who are guests in it
will find comfort,
company,
and composure—

so that friends will find in it
friendliness—

so that those who come to it with joy
will go from it with more joy,
and those who come troubled
will go feeling peace—

so that we who live in it
day and night and through the years
will find in it
quiet when we need quiet,
exercise of mind when we need that,
a shelter for body and spirit,
a place to spend solitary hours
and to share with those we love.

Amen.

Our Resolutions

Charles Fillmore

Out of the sordid, the base, the untrue,
Into the noble, the pure, and the new;
Out of all darkness and sadness and sin,
Spiritual harmonies to win.
   This is our resolution.

Out of all discord, toil, and strife,
Into a calm and perfect life;
Out of all hatred and jealous fear,
Into love's cloudless atmosphere.
   This is our resolution.

Out of the narrow and cramping creeds,
Into a service of loving deeds;
Out of a separate, limited plan,
Into the brotherhood of man.
   This is our resolution.

Out of our weakness to conscious power,
Wisdom and strength for every hour;
Out of our doubt and sore dismay,
Into the faith for which we pray.
    This is our resolution.

Out of the bondage of sickness and pain,
Out of poverty's galling chain;
Into the freedom of perfect health,
Into the blessings of endless wealth.
    This is our resolution.

Out of this fleeting mortal breath,
Out of the valley and shadow of death;
Into the light of the perfect way,
Into the freedom of endless day.
    This is our resolution.

Out of the finite sense of things,
Into the joy the infinite brings;
Out of the limits of time and space,
Into the boundless life of the race.
    This is our resolution.

I Behold the Christ in You

Frank B. Whitney

I behold the Christ in you,
  Here the life of God I see;
I can see a great peace too,
  I can see you whole and free.

I behold the Christ in you.
  I can see this as you walk;
I see this in all you do,
  I can see this as you talk.

I behold God's love expressed,
  I can see you filled with power;
I can see you ever blessed,
  See Christ in you hour by hour.

I behold the Christ in you,
  I can see that perfect one;
Led by God in all you do,
  I can see God's work is done.

Irradiance

Ernest C. Wilson

Oh, fill me with Thy presence, Lord,
  That love may shine through me
To quicken that same presence, Lord,
  In all whose eyes can see.

Oh, fill me with Thy presence, Lord,
  That wisdom may be mine
To share Thy light with all who need
  To let their own light shine.

Oh, fill me with Thy presence, Lord,
  To guide what power I wield,
That it may ever strengthen good,
  And be from ill a shield.

Oh, fill me with Thy presence, Lord—
  But need I longer wait?
Thy presence hath been given me,
  To live and radiate!

Blessing for a Marriage

James Dillet Freeman

May your marriage bring you all the exquisite excite-
  ments
  a marriage should bring,
  and may life grant you also patience, tolerance, and
  understanding.
May you always need one another—
not so much to fill your emptiness as to help you to know
  your fullness.
A mountain needs a valley to be complete;
  the valley does not make the mountain less but more;
and the valley is more a valley because it has a
  mountain towering over it.
So let it be with you and you.
May you need one another, but not out of weakness.
May you want one another, but not out of lack.
May you entice one another, but not compel one
  another.
May you embrace one another, but not encircle one
  another.

May you succeed in all important ways with one
      another,
   and not fail in the little graces.
May you look for things to praise, often say, "I love you!"
   and take no notice of small faults.
If you have quarrels that push you apart,
May both of you hope to have good sense enough to take
      the first step back.
May you enter into the mystery which is the awareness
    of one another's presence—
no more physical than spiritual, warm and near when
      you are side by side,
and warm and near when you are in separate rooms or
      even distant cities.
May you have happiness, and may you find it making
      one another happy.
May you have love, and may you find it loving one
      another!
        Thank You, God,
        for Your presence here with us
        and Your blessing on this marriage.
        Amen.

Poems of
Inspiration

Carousel

Jean S. Platt

Remember that ride on the carousel—
your first—and the endless wait
till the man came around and released the chain
that held you at the gate?
Remember, at last, astride the mount,
what rapture filled your soul
as the prancing steed went round and round
and up and down the pole?
And the lights were bright and the music sweet,
and when you were near the top,
you could see balloons and the crowds below
and wished it would never stop?

Oh, life is a glorious carousel,
and there's nothing to portend
(when the lights are bright and the music sweet)
that the ride will ever end.
So choose your charger, command him well,
observe; there is much to see.
What joy to be here on the carousel;
"Hosanna!" from you and from me.

Reflections

Ann Bregach

Pressing down upon the mind are the little things
That make one confused about what is right.
To be able to be diplomatic and never say the wrong
        thing;
Sometimes it seems so impossible!
But does it really make any difference?
Will one hundred years from now the effect of
What I have said today be of value?
Does the tiny pebble tossed so indifferently
Into the waters truly create a ripple that touches
Anyone? At all? And what if it does?
Who really cares?
Ah! One does. And that One is God.
God cares.
So! If I tend to think that it really doesn't matter,
If I am sensitive to a situation,
If I feel that it doesn't make a lot of sense
Or that I want to back off from an unpleasant task,
I must pause and reflect upon that thought.
If God cares, then *I am* responsible for that
Little ripple in the waters of the lives of
All whom I touch.
So it really is not a problem after all, for where I am
God is. That is all that matters!

In the Secret Place

James Dillet Freeman

I have imagined mountains
And waterfalls and trees
More beautiful than any
Anybody sees.

Earth's peaks may loom unclimbable,
But I can venture there,
And my mind-trees can blossom
When every tree is bare.

We all have secret valleys
Hidden in our heart;
And there, though all the world's at war,
Peace can start.

Knowing

Verle Bell

It is a point just beyond
   wondering, doubting, waiting;
A certainty that *now* is the time for
   a bud to uncurl;
An undeniable urge in the swallow
   that this is the instant to rise
     in flight toward the south;
A realization in the cells
   that *now* is the moment for
     a wound to begin to heal;
The moment when a soul decides it is time
   to move on to a new realm.
Knowing comes from within
   and cannot be denied.
Thank You, God, that I know You are,
     That I know You are love,
   And that I know I am Yours.

Demonstration

Margaret Finefrock

How thankful I am
that Jesus
did not stop at the point
of thoughtful solitude,
that Beethoven
could not keep his music
resounding in his head,
that King
was not content
merely to dream.

How grateful I am
for an infinite Presence
that moves mind
into action,
thoughts
into concreteness,
inspiration
into expression.

How beautiful I am
that I too
can sing the songs,
write the sonnets,
perform the dance
of my own being.

30

Revelation

Elizabeth Searle Lamb

The airplane
after takeoff
climbs quickly
through clouds
and suddenly
breaks through
into the joy
of sunshine.

So my spirit
prays through
a fog of doubt
and reaches
suddenly that
still place
where I know
the Oneness.

The sunshine
of joy
floods
my entire being.

The Sea and I

James Dillet Freeman

The sea is very deep
And stretches very wide;
The earth and heavens keep
Pulse with its pulsing tide.
But standing on my shore
I catch no less in me
A sense of more, yet more,
As of a mystery,
Of deeps I hardly know
And yet they are my own,
Where sometimes I can go
Alone, yet not alone,
And touch the boundless rim
Where I am one with Him.

Yet More

James Dillet Freeman

By looking at an acorn,
Small and hard and plain,
Could I conceive of oak trees?
By listening to rain,
Could I imagine oceans?
Or could I understand
The desert if my hand but held
A single grain of sand?
Then let me never think
That what I chance to see,
This face, this frame, these thoughts,
That this is all of me.
Yet more than ageless oaks
Or seas that have no shore,
In me there also is
Yet more, yet more.

Benediction

John M. Byrns, Jr.

You are My seed.
Within you I have placed all power.
Need I say more to prove
That limitless you are;
That through love, deed, and aspiration
You expand to reach a star?

Go forth My seed!
May the pent-up creativity within you
Burst the shell of time and space
And explode into the Truth
Of all you were meant to be
From the moment of creation.

I give you all.
If less you see
It is your self-developed shell
Which calls the cadence of captivity
And halts the flow of Spirit
Seeking to fly free!

Ocean Lore

Doris Hanks Enabnit

Deep and mysterious ocean
Where fathomless caverns roar,
You draw me with your greatness,
You speak of the evermore.

You breathe of the snow-clad mountains
And whisper of cedar and pine;
You drink of the hills and the valleys
With essence of woodland and vine.

What treasures from Earth's vast storehouse,
What substance of vision and dream
Are brought by the turbulent rivers
And the distant mountain stream.

What rhythm of tides and of seasons,
With neither beginning nor end,
Is forever taking and giving
In one eternal blend!

I Serve My Best

Leslie E. Dunkin

When friends forget and leave someone alone,
　When people hurl a bitter word or deed,
Where seeds of hate and jealousy are sown,
　I serve my best with love for those in need.

When troubles come as threatening storms assail,
　When paths grow steep and biting winds severe,
When doubts arise as human efforts fail,
　I serve my best with faith for those who fear.

I look within for wisdom, strength, and skill
　To see and meet all needs as they begin;
I have a clearer view, a stronger will;
　I serve my best and know I'll grow within.

Midnight Serenade

Doris E. Dodge

Out of the darkness at this midnight hour
   I hear a song that stills this subtle fear.
The sound is low, but yet its vivid power
   Repeats a startling vision to my ear,
And sends it soaring high upon the tower
   Of peaceful thought, much likened to a seer
That takes the job to map a forward course,
And prove it comes to guide from just one Source.

No more the darkness throws its ugly hiss,
   But stays within the bonds of fractured dreams;
Until the dawn and daylight kiss,
   I drink the song in eager draughts it seems,
And thus the passing moments fail to miss
   The hidden secrets of this One who schemes
That sorrow from its cloistered roots be torn,
Then joy in greatest measures will be born.

Always the Seer

John D. Engle, Jr.

It always is the seer
and never what is seen.
Though objects find
reflection in the eyes,
the mind alone
knows where the thought has been;
and only the intuitive
are wise.

It always is the hearer
and never what is heard.
Though all vibrations
activate the ear,
sound is an illusion;
and it never is the bird,
but awakened inward music
that we hear.

Ripples

Verle Bell

Scholars tell us
  that a stone,
    dropped into still water,
      causes ripples whose effect
      goes on eternally . . .
Their vibration never ceases.

Sages have said
  that one loving thought,
    cast into the sea of life,
      has infinite value . . .
Its vital waves go on
  and on and on, blending
    with other loving thoughts,
      strengthening, intensifying,
multiplying their immortal good.

I Want to Write a Sonnet

John D. Engle, Jr.

I want to write a sonnet that will sing
about the tree that waltzes with the wind.
I want to reach green syllables that will wing
their way into the wood to bow and bend.
I want to capture phrases that will dance,
paired with an unseen partner whose delight
is woven into wonders of romance
that keep all flowers in bloom, all birds in flight.
I want to fashion lines so delicate
the wind will welcome them, the leaves applaud,
lines so perfect they will elevate
the soul in gladness to the glow of God.
   I want to borrow bliss from wind and tree
   and let their beauty sing itself through me.

Immersed

John D. Engle, Jr.

Immersed in infinite energy and love,
I'm part of the eternal flow of things.
No matter when or where or how I move,
whether on earth with wheels or in air with wings,
I am a part of everything that is,
all that has been or will ever be.
Designed by the dreams of all divinities,
all beauty and all Truth are mixed in me.
Knowing this, I shed my shell of doubt,
till free in the freedom of the Mystic Mind
and linked to laws of love, I go about
fulfilling that for which I was designed,
   which is to sing myself and try to share
   the loveliness of which I am aware.

Deeps

James Dillet Freeman

We were not meant for bays and shallows, for
Safe sailing never out of sight of shore—
Men, mariners, oh, we were meant for more!
Ours are the deeps, the seas we do not know,
The seas where none before has dared to go,
The seas of faith where only strange winds blow.
Leaving known landfalls for the fainter-hearted,
To seek the undiscovered, the uncharted—
Where the vast voyage ended, there let ours be started!

Focus

Janna Russell

I am the gaze of God
into the meadow
going nowhere in particular
watching a multitude of daisies
sway in my love.
I declare this vision of nature
at peace with itself.

The Mystery

Glenn Clairmonte

Do I dare to presume that the Highest and Greatest
May bend to my level with precious advice?
Or is the whole cosmos already provided
With reasons to help me learn how to be wise?

The marvel of everyday living and loving
Surprises as joyful adventures unmask
The system established within the eternal,
And all that resounds is, "How can you ask?"

He Lives in Me

Jim Rosemergy

I sleep in His peace.
I wake in His joy.
I walk in His light,
And am warmed by His love.
And all that I am and will ever be
Is all because He lives in me.

Rivers Hardly Ever

James Dillet Freeman

Rivers hardly ever run in a straight line.
Rivers are willing to take ten thousand meanders
And enjoy every one
And grow from every one—
When they leave a meander
They are always more
Than when they entered it.
When rivers meet an obstacle,
They do not try to run over it;
They merely go around—
But they always get to the other side.
Rivers accept things as they are,
Conform to the shape they find the world in—
Yet nothing changes things more than rivers;
Rivers move even mountains into the sea.
Rivers hardly ever are in a hurry—
Yet is there anything more likely
To reach the point it sets out for
Than a river?

My Friend

Marsha Graf

My friend,
you have melted off years of
plaster
and exposed the adobe bricks
within me.
You have freed me from
self-deception
by seeing through the
smoke screen
with which I have surrounded
my heart.
You have taught me the meaning
of love,
and I am growing because
of you.
Thank you. You are truly
my friend.

Out of the Mists

James Dillet Freeman

When the mists blow across my soul
On the way to where I am going,
And I have no way of knowing
What way the waves may roll
Or how the wind is blowing,
And I catch no certain shore
Or light out there for seeing,
Then the light that I look for
Is the light of my own being—
O dear dear inward light
Beyond all understanding,
A surer guide than sight
To lead me through the night
And bring me to safe landing.

Myrtle

Joanne L. Stanley

Fragile lady,
Lovely flower.
Fragile petals
Open before my eyes.
I see yesterday, and all time
That is free.
She fills the Village ether
With loving allness,
Blending in a sunset
Generation to generation
Of rose fragrance.

The Man, the Shore, the People

Mildred N. Hoyer

A haunting thought refuses
To be stilled, and with the thought
Comes an imagining, an unborn wish, perhaps,
That through a modern miracle
Of inner space all peoples of our planet
Might appear once more upon the shore
Of Galilee, and listen.

Reality returns, at least in part:
We see again our peopled shore; we see
The Speaker as before, His voice the same,
With words of power to stem the coming tide,
With words to strengthen and to guide.

Oh, stay and listen!

Messenger

Jane Priest

I sat one morning silently
to listen for my Lord,
hands in my lap cupped quietly
as if to catch His Word.

And as His holy hush came down
to lift my heart above,
on velvet paws a kitten came
and filled my hands with love.

47

God's Sunsets

Pauline Havard

You should gather one of God's sunsets occasionally;
Not by glancing out of a car as you rush by,
But on foot, pausing—the longer the better.
You should garner the colors
As you would flowers growing in a field.
For what are sunsets
But Indian paintbrush and goldenrod
In the meadow of the sky?
It is your privilege to pick at random
While the colors last;
To carry back to your quiet room
A sheaf of red and gold from this mass of bloom.

The Mantle

Mildred N. Hoyer

In the midst of a multitude
Or alone
Within a solitary room,
Waking or sleeping,
Sorrowing or rejoicing,
Hopeless or hope-filled,
In the cathedral
Or in the marketplace;
Always,
The unseen Presence,
Enveloping us
With the protecting mantle
Of love.

48

Transformation

Pauline Havard

With the white impersonality of snow
Distinctions are wiped out, and all is beauty.
And it is like this when love rules the heart—
All people seem the same, no matter what race or creed;
All shine with the same look: divinity.
When prejudice is ousted, and we love
Without reservation, a change takes place;
We view all mankind as it really is,
Made in His image. And just as the pure snow,
God's silver gift, transforms our outer world,
So love transforms our secret inner world,
And hope adds its dazzle, its snow-light,
As hearts, loved, give off their own kind of glow.

Discovery

Marsha Graf

Out of the
coldest
and seemingly most
barren
times of our lives,
we discover
hidden truths
and bring them as
gifts
into the lives of
others.

Accord

Janna Russell

Close to the beating heart of the universe
Warm, as within the womb of life itself
Loving, as if comforted beyond mere pleasure,
The consciousness of eternal goodness is peace.
This beautiful grace is ours to share.

To a Friend

Jim Rosemergy

There was a time when I thought
    God walked beside you,
But now I see God moves
    with every step you take.

There was a time when I thought
    God loved you,
But now I feel you are the love
    I often speak of.

There was a time when I thought
    God had blessed you
But now I know you
    are His blessing for me.

Trinities

Ric Schumacher

We are
Intricate beings comprised
Of countless trinities.
Each trinity
Is but a part
Of the great cantata
Of life.

The nineteenth century
Strings sing
Spirit, soul, body,
Mind, idea, expression.

The modern timpani bellows
Superego, id, ego,
Neocortex, limbic, R-complex.

The ancient woodwinds whisper
Energy, light, form,
Thought, word, deed,

The timeless horns resound
Living, dying, rebirthing,
Old, young, eternal.

The heavenly Conductor
Raps His baton
And the music
Is played as
Triunal man.

Full Circle

Jean S. Platt

The old man sleeps—an embryo—
knees drawn up to his chest,
I hesitate to waken him;
perhaps it might be best
to let him dream a little yet;
he looks so peaceful there,
and life is so confusing now,
the happy moments, rare.

But even as I stand and watch,
he wakes to gaze at me.
No recognition on his face,
he stares; then suddenly
he beckons with a fragile hand
to bring me to his side.
(He wants someone to comb his hair;
he hasn't lost his pride.)

I hold the mirror when I'm through;
he's pleased; his hair looks fine.
Three score—the years I've been his child;
now, for a while, he's mine.

Out of the Primal Fire

Dennis Neagle

Out of the primal fire of the flesh
Uprisings of volcanic violence
Strive their blind way lifeward.
Coded harbingers of downward divinity
Seek to take, to break the sacred circle
And in their dark entombment of the womb, begin a
      brain.

Deep in the midnight darkness of the brain
Sparks the synaptic match
And so for a mystic moment
Ancient lines perpetually parallel
Merge, and upon their plane (impossibly)
Birth multi-dimensional thought.

Somewhere beyond the fingered grasp, a thought
Awaits extending itself beyond time's reach
Somewhere beyond coordinates of time and space
A Mind imposes its infinite will.
Something to be born below is known above—
And in the beginning darkness the Light is good.

Unity

Marcus Bach

What is Unity?
It is the word of Christ made new again,
The spirit of Christ reborn again;
The will of Christ revealed again,
The mind of Christ restored again;
It is the faith of Christ renewed again,
The law of Christ affirmed again,
The love of Christ employed again
To help man know himself again
The Self that is one with God.

In Sight

Joanne L. Stanley

How silently the sun sets,
Yet, how surely it will rise anew.
It has shining to do elsewhere
Before returning to our view.
Do we lament its loss,
Or are we confident of its return?

Would that we were so sure
Of the Christ-Son-Light within us,
Certain that it, too, shines on.
Look to it! Listen to it! Let it glow!
For its brilliance and warmth never set.
Afar and near, the Christ-Son is always in sight.

Ongoing

R. H. Grenville

In spring-gambol youth,
like a foal in a meadow,
I was impatient to be
what I've since become.
Then a shadow
touched all vistas the morning light
once held:
foreboding shiver of the concept,
"old."

So I went out to clear my thought
in the clear air,
under a sky
older than I;
passed a tree
on a road
to a lake by a mountain,
all older than I;
saw the day crowned
with that special exuberance of delight
called sunset,
which Adam himself must have thrilled to,
and felt life's vast
continuity.

What's a shadow to those who carry
their own light?
I'm not young or old or in-between.
I'm me!

Room Consecration

Jim Rosemergy

In this room
grows the tree of life
and from it come
the fruits of health and wholeness.

In this room
is the spring of living water
which drowns the cry of death
and drains its power.

In this room
echoes the heartbeat of love
and from it resound
acts of kindness,
words of understanding.

In this room
lies the hidden manna
which falls from heaven
and gives spiritual nourishment.

In this room
dawns the morning star
which guides all who enter here
to a new heaven,
a new Earth.

In this room
hangs the mirror of the soul
in which we see
what we truly are . . .
sons of the Most High.

In this room
is the throne of God
and from it come
power and dominion
to those present.

In this room
hangs the yoke of Christ
and with it comes
the strength
to bear all burdens.

In this room
dwells God,
the Father of us all.

God Spoke to Me

William Arthur Ward

Through the song of a bird
He announced His presence.
Through a golden sunrise
He shared some of His splendor.
Through a season of silence
He called me His child.
Through His word of Truth
He told me the Way.
Through the smile of a friend
He revealed His nature.
Through the eyes of an infant
He expressed His joy.
Through the sparkle of raindrops
He spoke of a miracle.
Through my time of indecision
He gave me the answer.

Poems for
Spiritual Guidance

Reaching Out

Winifred Brand

My spirit wants to reach
and stretch and grow,
to go beyond the fears and hunger
and the disillusions
of the world we know.
And yet I know
it cannot reach
and stretch
and grow
beyond the aching of the soul,
until it takes
the fears
the hopes
the tears
the doubts and shattered dreams
unto itself,
resolving every one
in its own way
and reaching first
the Christ within.

To a Doubtful Dreamer

John D. Engle, Jr.

Introduce all your dreams
to the world.
Let it know
that you dream
while awake.
You will find
that the sky
is unfurled
as the Earth is aglow
for your sake.

There is space
for your name
in the sky.
There is soil
for your roots
in the Earth.
Hold fast to your dreams
nor deny
that dreams
were your reason for birth.

Lovest Thou Me?

Hettie Wallace

You say you love Me as you've loved no other,
And swear all loves beside grow pale and dim.
Yet loving Me, should you not love your brother,
Knowing that I am also a part of him?

You love the blush of sunset and of morning,
Blue radiant skies on distant mountain peaks,
The song of birds that waken you at dawning,
The hurrying river as the sea it seeks.

The breath of flowers makes your Earth an Eden,
Each lovely bloom a perfect work of art,
The love and faith that in each dog lies hidden,
A moonlit night that thrills you to the heart.

All these and more you love because of Me,
My Presence in all nature you can find,
And yet in him, My image, you can see
Naught but a man and to the God are blind.

Full of faults of thoughts, words, and deeds is he,
But greater is the essence of My Being
Which now and throughout eternity
Is one with him—Oh! Be not so unseeing.

Look with the eyes of love, and realize
My Presence in each erring son of Mine.
Man at his worst is still an angel in disguise,
And at his best, one with Me—and divine.

Only by loving the Christ in him can you
Fulfill the law which is and e'er shall be,
The law which separates the false from true,
And proves *there's nothing in it all but Me.*

Paths

R. H. Grenville

Paths
interest me.
They have a jaunty
and adventurous air.
Not one runs straight.
They go
the curving, easy way
that rivers flow,
yet, inevitably,
arrive somewhere.

Paths
are a kind of trust
that someone had,
being the first
to get from here to there,
unanxious and unhurried.
Hearts move that way for
those who journey inward
on the path of prayer.

Revival

R. H. Grenville

Walking through morning grass
I left my mark:
a wake of stems crushed flat.
Of course, I meant no harm.
So often, life's like that,
and hopes get brushed aside,
feelings are hurt.

But the resilient grass
bore me no grudge.
By evening light,
the sun-absorbing blades
stood full upright.

I, too, can draw on strengths
beyond the seen
to spring up like the grass,
refreshed and green;
after some heedless word
or ill wind blowing,
to reaffirm my faith
and keep on growing.

The Shell

Jim Rosemergy

Limit to the limitless,
Protector of the past,
Unneeded guide of the yet unborn,
Shell of ignorance, broken by the light,
   Blind child of light, staggered by the freedom
   Yet free to build another shell or
   Free to live in light.

Healing Comes Quietly

Leona Hayes Chunn

Healing is a quiet thing.
It does not descend upon the seeker
With loud acclaim;
No fanfare heralds its approach.
With faith its counterpart,
Healing comes quietly,
Working its benediction like holy air,
In gentleness,
Through avenues of prayer.

Unity If

Nita Buckley

If I can know that God is omnipotent
   When others doubt that He is true,
If I can touch that part of God within me
   And see the Christ abide in others too,
If I can pray and not be tired by prayer,
   Or, being weary, not begin to doubt,
If the candle of my faith begins to flicker
   And I can keep the flame from going out,
If I can draw upon sustaining power
   To help me cope and meet my needs each day.
If I can be a comfort and give guidance
   And help another person find his way,
If I can tap the knowledge of omniscience
   And reach into the heart of Divine Mind,
If I can ease the grief of someone hurting
   And offer words of hope for all mankind,
If I can walk with the corrupt without corruption
   And see God where it seems that evil lies,
If I can stand with courage and decision
   And keep the goal steadfast before my eyes,
If I can fill a heavy heart with laughter
   And recognize that joy is mine to share
And see the pattern of my highest good unfolding,
   I'm living in my Father's loving care.

The Teacher

Pamela Yearsley

Those who would be teachers, know this:
If your heart is set upon generously sharing with others
your own knowledge, thereby somehow to enhance their
      lives,
then know that your gift will not succeed.

For a true teacher does not seek to instill in others
her or his understanding and knowledge;
rather, a true teacher seeks to be an instrument
to stimulate the student's own wisdom.

Do not seek to inspire others; seek to be inspired.
Only by being inspired can you bring inspiration.
For inspiration is not a gift we can give to another.
It is a state of being that magnifies itself in others.

Therefore, feel not downhearted
because in your own ecstacy of inspiration
others do not seem to share.
Instead, hold steady in your way—
in your own state of being—
and be inspired.

Partake lavishly of your experience
and hold no expectations of others doing so.
In their own time, in their own way
will they feast at the same table.
But let not pride take your hand and lord it over their
        heads.

Let not your students be to you as the moon
whose light is but a reflection.
But let them be as the stars
whose brilliance shows forth of their own nature.
This is the gift of the teacher.

The Last Place I Had Thought to Seek

Rebecca Lynn Gregory

The gentlest of spirits is the God that I have found.
So long I sought for Him upon far distant skies and
  grounds.
The last place I had thought to seek was here within my
  heart.
How could a God, I reasoned, be with my dark soul a
  part?

For I looked in a twisted glass and thought it finely
  made,
and doubted not the warped reflection of myself it gave,
until a loving Force reached out to shatter that dark
  mirror
and place within my shaking hands an image true and
  clear.

So there within that unknown Self I found the Lord I
  sought—
the fire of my being, all of calm and mercy wrought.
Now I need look no further for a God that I might see,
but I shall live to make my God full manifest in me.

The Bee and the Butterfly

R. H. Grenville

"So much to do in a clover field!"
hums the bee.
So much to do! a familiar theme,
it seems to me,
watching the pollen-dusted fellow dart
from wild lupin to smiling daisy-heart.

And now a butterfly in gold and brown
settles before me on a clover crown—
a plump pink cushion for the weary one
in silent gratitude to rest upon.

Wings folded, it remains
in passive state.
Sleeping? or does a monarch meditate?
"Weary not with well-doing," drones the bee
with zealot zest.
"Come ye apart," signals the butterfly,
"and rest."

The good advice each gives me echoes in
my listening heart—
the beat-pause rhythm of life's vital art.

I Caught This Morning at Dawning

Dennis Neagle

I caught this morning at dawning,
And the sun on the last night's snow
Revealed that there was no footfall—
Only the soft silent flow
Of Earth and Earth's undulations,
And the white unbroken snow.

This is our soul at each dawning,
Silent and perfectly white,
Unblemished it follows our contours
As if somehow God's delight
Is to cover us softly with mercy,
And renew us over the night.

Open Your Hand

Dorothy R. Fulton

Truth, like a mysterious, silken cat,
eludes one's anxious grasp, yet comes
silent and unbeckoned to the
motionless lap of a quiet soul.

Love, like a fragile bubble from a child's pipe,
is broken by the anxious grasp, yet settles its
delicate rainbows gently on an
outstretched, open hand.

Peace, the silent presence holding Truth,
the warm wind that carries love, cannot be grasped,
for it is in us, and around us, yet beyond us—
our beginning, our conveyance, and our journey's end.

Cognizance

R. H. Grenville

The inner Self,
near to me,
dear to me—
the radiant deathless Self,
becomes more and more
clear to me
as I turn my attention
more and more frequently
to the enfolding,
interpenetrating,
limitless divine reality
that *is* me
in my child-of-God
capacity to be
victorious,
loving,
understanding,
joyous,
and free!

On Flying

Ric Schumacher

If you would have wings,
Stand guard
At the gate
Of your mind.

If you would soar,
Walk hand in hand
With your brother
And your God.

If you would fly high,
Swim deep
In the waters
Of your heart and soul.

Love and wisdom
Are your wings,
And their right use
Will carry you beyond the clouds of limitation.

Beautiful Words

Glenn Clairmonte

Arrayed like the lilies and winged like the birds
And sweet as the south wind are beautiful words.
Your words become beautiful when they express
The things that you wish for the people you bless.
You, too, can resemble the lilies and birds
Whenever you speak, if you think of your words.

Choice

Sandra L. Hill

It awes me still
that the exact same "reality"
can construct a hell or heaven unfold,
awaiting only my decision.
That undelegatable and inescapable
choice between skywinged freedom
and those airless, narrow tunnels
in the marrow of the mind.
Amazing! A different evaluation
gives a different destination
every time.

76

Within the Depths of Me

Kalar Walters

The heights I reach, the worlds I touch,
   the wonders that I dream of,
Or all the things I ever wished
   or ever could conceive of
Are things beyond, and things below,
   and things that cannot be,
Except for those that live and grow
   within the depths of me,
So very deep and hidden that,
   save for times like these,
I can only dream of them
   and wish that they could be
A thing apart, a thing alive,
   a thing that I could see,
A thing to touch, a thing to hold,
   a thing to comfort me.
But if I watch, and if I wait,
   and hold to all that's true,
There will come a time, and then a place,
   and what I'll see is You.
For You are what I dream of,
   the things that cannot be,
Except for those that live and grow
   within the depths of me.

Levels

Virginia Scott Miner

The old pine's going, I thought.
Its branches each year seem less full,
more light shows through.

But, from the second floor,
when I looked out into it,
the branches seemed fuller,
and each twig was tipped in green—
bright and new-growth green—
and I thought,
It is growing, growing still.

So much depends on
the level at which we stand.

Poems for
Spiritual Upliftment

Life Is Neither Born Nor Does It Die

Jim Rosemergy

*A man who had lost his family in a
disaster was asked about life and death.
This was his answer:*

If you say the sunrise marks the birth of day
    and sunset marks its death,
    you mark yourself a fool.

It is the rising sun that bears the day,
    and the setting sun the night.
    Neither dies, but both are born.

If the sun rises upon a man
    and you call it birth,
    and sets and you call it death,
    you call yourself a fool.

Life is neither born nor does it die.
It is like the air we breathe:
    It is there but cannot be seen.
It is like the breeze that stirs the leaves:
    It is gentle and moving, strong yet touching.
It is like the dew upon a rose:
    It clings, yet does not bind.

It speaks with the voice of silence,
    yet you always answer the call.
It stands beside you and dwells within you.
It brings you a gift and bears you a child.
The gift is God, and the child is you.

Lifted by Prayer

Winifred Heiskell Layton

Today I watched a hummingbird
bore into a bead of honeysuckle bloom
that drapes like tassles of macramé
in my summer outdoor living room.

    I know the whirring of those tiny wings
    suspended in midair
    is exactly the way my every thought
    suspends itself in prayer.

Unseen the force that keeps blurred wings
treading air with velocity.
The same unseen power is mine, is mine—
surging to buoy the soul of me.

According to Appearance

R. H. Grenville

Another sunset ends the day.
The firebird nests in plumes of gold.
Light from the Earth has fled away.
As our ancestors used to say:
the sun has died, and all is gray.
But it is we who turn away.
How often, in the soul's deep night,
do we unjustly blame the Light.

I Am That I Am

Hettie Wallace

That which says "I"
In all the purity of Truth,
Knows that I cannot die,
Knows that eternal life, eternal youth,
Radiant as dawn's bright promise
Of a glorious day, are mine—
Mine is the bliss of knowing this,
I am a being divine.

The Next Ascent

Joan H. Ward

Aging
is like a rose
clinging to the bud of youth
until
the petals of understanding unfold
and ascend to a radiant bloom.

The rose
pauses in glorious consummation—
then surrenders to the Creator
only to pause
in timelessness again
before the next ascent.

Life Wish

Virginia Bird Helms

Not half in love with death, not I
Not while the robin sings
Clear-throated in the dawn.
Never while the apple tree
Stands like a bride in white,
Letting her veil flow down around her
To the ground.

How could I bear to search the sky
And never see the moon through tracery
Of leaves and branches laced before it,
Or never wake to muted snow, with small wild creatures
Kicking up a sunlit, glittering dust?

Perhaps in time I'll learn to say good-bye,
And never once look back,
Lest I see Thy lambent maples
Glowing redly in the light, and all my courage vanish.
But wait. It may be all this beauty is but shadow,
True substance yet to come.
If I can only steel my heart to lose
What I would hold close-fisted,
And trust Thy promise—then, Thy will be done.

Thesis

William Walter De Bolt

Death is not a period
bringing the sentence of life to a close
like the spilling of a moment
or the dissolution of an hour.

Death is a useful comma
which punctuates, and labors to convince
of more to follow.

Eulogy for a Neighbor's Son

Jean S. Platt

I thought the early morning mine
that day in June so long ago,
until I heard him call his dog;
then, seated on the patio,
I saw him dance across the yard,
the grass still wet with dew. What joy
to watch him, unobserved, and know
the ecstasy of one small boy!

His life, so brief, was not to have
an afternoon or evening; still
he loved the morning, so he danced
and, in my memory, always will.

What Is Love?

Verle Bell

Love is the sun and the rain
   kissing the bud into bloom.
Love is the flower
   giving its fragrant beauty
     to the air.
Love is the dropping
   of the petals
   into the good soil
     to feed it
     with their joy.
Love is the openhearted receiving
   of the earth,
and its giving again
   to the new seeds
   which fall therein.
Love is being what
   God created us to be.
Love is being at peace
   with all humanity,
     with all creation.
   Love is being one with God.

Vision

Ernest C. Wilson

If life should seem to falter,
  If friends should seem to fail,
I would not bid Thee alter
  The things 'gainst which I rail;
But cleanse, O God, my vision
  That I may clearly see,
Through senses that imprison,
  The good Thou hast for me.

The Need for Acceptance

John D. Engle, Jr.

Sometimes I dull the voice that speaks through me
by my doubt and my ineptitude.
Sometimes the song that wishes to be free
is locked in pain by my discordant mood.
Sometimes the beauty that surrounds me waits
in vain for my belated recognition.
And sometimes when awareness hesitates,
truth mocks the petty ends of my ambition.
Sometimes I allow complexity
to rob me of the simple songs of nature;
and yet I may hold heaven next to me
if I proclaim my right as heaven's creature.
  God's kingdom is eternal and divine.
  If I accept it, He will make it mine.

Eternal Love

Janna Russell

Spheres of light
in unbroken rhythm
wrap me around with new heaven.
My sense is translucent,
and it is now
a softened, lulling eternity.

Inside
I am as sudden and whole
as a moment of lingering joy.
To radiate a word of this pearl
is to honor
the manner of loving.

Starless Night

Henrietta Liebknecht

There is a promise
Even in the quiet beauty
Of a starless night
    When wing of bird is still,
    Secure in nest.
Man stands alone
Inbreathing silence,
    Knowing dawn and light
    Follow night's unrest.

Why Must We Die?

Pauline Olson

Heavenly Father, Most High,
Tell this child,
Why must we die?

Little boy, the fire dies out,
but smoke ascends and passes
from your sight; the stars are
there by day as surely as
the night.
Young eyes can read the promise
hid in all living things;
already you know, better than I,
that you never really die.
The serpent sheds its skin,
the caterpillar spreads great
wings, and both return no more
to yearn for things
          outgrown.

New Life

Verle Bell

Like the seed which is placed
into the dark earth
to shed its shell
that it may respond to the sun
with green shoots;

Like the waves which have collapsed
against the rocks
that they may spring again
to new heights;

Like the sun which sets
that it may rise
on new horizons;

So death will always be
the gateway
to new Life.

The Doubter

John D. Engle, Jr.

He climbed bravely toward the stars of night,
lit his candle from a star and held it high.
And, as he descended from that height,
he was followed by descending sky.
The sky came down with him and rested on
the mountain peak. And, though the stars retained
their places, they grew dim till they were gone.
Only he, his candle, and the sky remained.
Now he was the center and the sun.
He, the hub; the universe, a wheel.
"It is not true," he said; "I have begun
to dream too much. These things cannot be real."
  And as he spoke, this merest breath of doubt
  became the storm that blew his candle out.

Discovery

John D. Engle, Jr.

Rowing out
of my stream
of dream
to explore reality,
I find
reality is
but a deeper dream
that flows
from a larger lake
of Mind.

90

Infinity

Frances Elliott

Where does my life reach its end, O God?
Is it at my feet as they trod
O'er Thy lovely land? Or as I touch
With eager fingertips so very much
Of Thy goodness everywhere? Or yet
At height of head held up to Thee to get
The glories of Thy graciousness?
I cannot see the end, O God,
For where finality would be
Is always infancy.

Within Us, Too

R. H. Grenville

Strike a match,
light a candle
or a pyre—
always the same
bright pyramid of fire
leaps into being—
tongues of red and gold
reach up, whichever way you hold
taper or torch.
Within us, too, something
born to aspire,
a yearning, upward burning
spirit-fire.

Eternal Vision

J. Sig Paulson

They know me not
who think that I am
   only flesh and blood—
   a transient dweller
   on the fragile spaceship earth
   that gave me human birth.
For I am Spirit:
   eternal, indestructible, not confined to space or time,
   and when my sojourn here is through,
   my roles fulfilled, my assignments done,
   I will lay aside this space suit called my body
   and move on to other mansions, roles, assignments
   in our Father's house of eternal life.
So dry your tears;
   weep not overmuch for me—nor for yourself.
   Set me free
   in the love that holds us all
   and makes us one eternally.
   Our paths will cross again.
   Our minds and hearts will touch.
   Our souls will shout with joy and laughter
As we recall
   the lives we've lived,
   the worlds we've seen,
   the ways we've trod
   to find ourselves—at last—in God.

Release

Irma Oestmann

I wanted to hold you, thinking that holding was loving,
But soon I learned that this was not true love; and so
I let go. It's called release.
You are now free to waft on the winds of your soul.
I watch you as you move into new worlds.
My heart is happy for your freedom and mine.
Momentarily I long to hold you again as you touch my
    branch,
Ever so lightly, on your wind-blown path.
The touch reminded me of tender moments we had
    shared,
Of tears and of laughter.

Now you are choosing a new way of thinking and living.
Yes, the choice is yours; and if you choose to light upon
    my
Branch again, momentarily, it shall be as the touch of
    eternity.
For now I know that we are both free spirits, free to do
    and
Free to be and especially free to be more together than
    apart.
For the soul and life in the branch are the same as in the
    leaf.
Our words are the same though many miles apart.
I wish you happy freedom; and, together or apart, our
    love is eternal,
More lasting and fulfilled now than before when we held
    so tightly.
Now we know true love and the releasing was the real
    beginning.

Variations on a Life

Janet Verkuyl

Soft tree with moods from golds to green,
deep grass, small bird—alive, unseen,
champagne the day—white clouds, a breeze,
yet death stood by, a life to seize.

As close he stood, as we both stared,
Death said, "I come, my work prepared."
"I've touched his body, bone, and hand,
I've felled the timber from its stand."

I said to Death, "The man is there.
You cannot touch him anywhere,
for sun is spilling through your night,
and he is heading for the light,
That part of him will always be—
You've only set a traveler free."

Poetic Meditations

This Quiet Place

Dorothy Pierson

I came to this quiet place
And found You waiting for me, God.
I hadn't heard You call,
I had no seeming need at all,
But I just felt guided to be still . . .
And here You are!

My heart is open to Your will.
Speak to me, God,
For I am listening within myself.
I hear You in my mind,
A kind of moving
As in the quiet of a forest,
Pleasant sounds, soft and whispering
To my heart.
In this place apart, O God,
Thank You for the peace I feel,
The sure knowing that You are here,
And real,
And that we are one
In this quiet place.

Secret Place

R. H. Grenville

At the heart of the cyclone,
stillness.
At the deep, dim heart of the sea,
stillness.

Am I less than sea and cyclone
that the heart of me
should be twisted and torn
in the cyclone whirl of events,
cast adrift on turbulent tides
of emotion and thought?

Oh, so it seemed, until
I went deep enough to find
the timeless untroubled Self
at the heart of my heart and mind:
beyond will and willfulness,
peace that is balm;
a holy solitude,
a healing calm.

Centered

R. H. Grenville

Before me and around me, nothing.
Below me and above me, nothing.
I am as new as the dawn's breaking.
Awareness becomes infinity, without horizons.
I am the Self I do not know,
that has known me forever.
Seated in the sky of emptiness
we merge our stillness.

Still Silence

Rebecca Lynn Gregory

Still silence calms the depths of me.
It sets my heart and spirit free,
and lights those paths which I thought gray
and misted as a gloomy day.
Within this deepest silence lie
the how and when, the where, the why,
and all the many answers sought
by years of forced and twisted thought.
The silence is my stillness—peace—
a fragrant, velvet-soft release;
a place within which I might touch
whene'er the world becomes too much.

A Process of Renewal

Elizabeth Searle Lamb

I relax.
I relax and release
all fear, all limitation.
I release all tension.
I release and let go.
I let go of the past—
inner as well as outer—
let all the past be past.
I let go and let God.
I let God infill me
with the universal life,
the one creative substance.
I make the letting in
of this life energy
the way of my life,
the way for all time
and for all need:
a strengthening
for all weakness,
an enriching
for all lack,
a healing for all
that is less
than the truth of being.
I relax;
I relax and release;
I release and let go;
I let go and let God.
And I rejoice
in the flowering
of my own re-formation.

In Meditation

Stahr Pope

I see and hear the rippling, clear,
   cool water,
   dancing freely to and fro—
   the spheres of the universe
   singing in the star-filled sky.

I feel
   the warmth of the night
   with its arms around me,
   and I am safe and at peace.

This very moment,
   I feel a rebirth
   within my whole being.

The melody of my soul
   picks up the tones
   of the universe;
   and it says:

I AM, I AM
   Peace, be still.
   I AM
   and always shall be,
   Time without end!

For Healing

R. H. Grenville

Come, step into the pool
of quietness.
Relax your tired heart.
Let silence bless
and ease your every part
to tranquil trust,
washing away all trace
of wearying dust.
This quiet holds the calm
of silken seas.
Enter it gratefully
and take your ease.
An angel Presence
ministers to all
who seek
this timeless place.
Her name is Peace.

Prayer Poems

Prayer

Jeanne Allen

I have prayed many kinds of prayers—

I have prayed in grateful silence,
my heart overflowing for answered
prayer.

I have prayed in frantic desperation
for the fulfillment of a need.

I have prayed in questions, seeking
wisdom and understanding.

I have prayed with true love in my
heart for another, wanting only the
highest and best for him.

I have prayed wordless prayers,
unable to verbalize my innermost
thoughts and feelings.

I have prayed prayers of many words,
singing hosannas as the psalms of
David.

And yet, in every kind of prayer I pray,
the Presence that is within me remains
the same. Always the light and love and
peace of God rush in to embrace my soul
when I pray. No matter what outer form
my prayer may take, I am brought closer
to God as I pray it.

Space Prayer

John D. Engle, Jr.

You are my Sun; I am Your satellite.
You are the Center around which I must whirl.
Your gravity keeps me orbiting day and night
in a vast and endless cosmic curl
of mist and motion, light and heat.
You bless me with Your beauty as I fly,
holding me near, but not too near. The beat
of angel wings I hear as they pass by
on heavenly maneuvers, and I feel
in the presence of such pure divinity
that I at last know what I know is real—
that I exist for You and You for me
and that we both exist to make love shine
till all men learn their purpose is divine.

God's Symphony

Mildred N. Hoyer

Oh, may it be played
    through me;
May I be
    an instrument
In His orchestra
    of life,
Playing the theme
    of the universe.

Make Me a Blessing, Lord

James Dillet Freeman

Make me a blessing, Lord! Help me
To help those needing help, to be
A blessing to my fellow men.
Instruct me when to speak and when
To hold my speech, when to be bold
In giving and when to withhold;
And if I have not strength enough,
Then give me strength. Lord, make me tough
With my own self but tender toward
All others. Let there be outpoured
On me the gentleness to bless
All who have need of gentleness.
Give me a word, a touch to fill
The lonely life, faith for the ill,
And courage to keep hearts up though
My own is feeling just as low.
When men have bitter things to meet
And quail and would accept defeat,
Then let me lift their eyes to see
The vision of Thy victory.
Help me to help; help me to give
The wisdom and the will to live!

This Day's Prayer

Elizabeth Searle Lamb

Dear God, on this day
help me to be open
to every experience.
I would feel the warmth
of sun, the chill of rain;
I would hear birdsong
and that other sound
which is an inner sound
by which I connect,
at times, with You.
I would see anew
the uncurling leaf
and the smile of a child
and the color of grape.
I would be aware of every
fragrance—sweet, pungent.
Oh dear God, I would be
centered firmly within
and so enabled to perceive
the patterns of Your world,
the world that holds me
for this time and space.

Great Emotions

Jack Tobin

Give me more patience
With child-like faith
For the ill-endowed.

Give me more feeling
In misunderstandings,
To erase pain.

Give me the sympathy
To pity a person
Who is hate consumed,
For his is a sickness
Greater than mine.

Give me more humor,
For smiles are contagious
With friendly results.

Give me more wisdom
To encourage and teach
The quality of tolerance.

Give me encompassing love,
The greatest emotion
That unites all eternity.

A Student's Prayer

James E. Sweaney

Lord, grant me now an open mind,
    Receptive, eager, quick to learn
The truths my teachers would impart;
    Give me the wisdom to discern

The right from wrong; give me the power
    To concentrate; give me Your sure,
Strong light of Truth to guide my way
    Through passages that seem obscure;

And let me know that You are near
    When I must go to face a test;
Erase my every thought of fear;
    Help me, Lord, to do my best.

Bless my teachers. Speak through them
    In clear and loving words and give
Them the selfless joy that comes
    From having helped a soul to live.

Help me retain what I have learned
    And use the wisdom I possess
To reach my goal, to build a life
    Of service and of happiness.

A Mini-Prayer

Elizabeth Searle Lamb

Dear God,
You are
my freedom
no matter
what bars
seem to
hold me back;
You are
my potential
even when
I seem to make
no progress;
You are
my challenge
to growth.

The Gift

Winifred Brand

God, thank You for the gift of words . . .
the giving and receiving;
the looking into others' hearts . . .
the blessing of believing.
God, thank You for the gift of words,
for thoughts that lift and linger . . .
the gift that blesses each alike,
the listener and the singer.

Gates of Dawn

Doris Hanks Enabnit

Give me the faith of bird that sings
Before the dawn has come,
That feels the day must surely break
Though the night be wild and dark.
So may it be when I must leave
This world that I have loved,
To behold the opening gates of dawn
Within the sunset's glow.

Morning Prayer

Ella Syfers Schenck

Lord, in the quiet of this morning hour,
I come to Thee for peace, for wisdom, power
To view the world today through love-filled eyes;
Be patient, understanding, gentle, wise.
To see beyond what seems to be, and know
Thy children as Thou knowest them; and so
Nought but the good in anyone behold.
Make deaf my ears to slander that is told;
Silence my tongue to aught that is unkind;
Let only thoughts that bless dwell in my mind.
Let me so kindly be, so full of cheer,
That all I meet may feel Thy presence near.
O clothe me in Thy beauty, this I pray,
Let me reveal Thee, Lord, through all the day.

Father, I Know You

Jim Rosemergy

Father, I know You
> to be so large as to be
> a part of everything
And yet small enough
> to feel every heartbeat
> and know every human sigh.

Father, I know You
> to govern a universe
And yet You allow me
> to live my life of learning.

Father, I know You
> to dwell in the strangest places,
> on the high road . . .
> and where I cannot go
And yet you live within me
> in a dwelling place
That you call home.

Father, thank You
> that I may know
> that You are there
> wherever I might go.

Be Thou Made Whole

R. H. Grenville

In quiet periods of prayer
we feel the healing Presence near
and words Jesus spoke in Galilee
are spoken to us inwardly.
  Be thou made whole!
  Be thou complete:
  clear, active mind,
  strong, agile feet;
  blood flowing free
  to every part;
  sound, limber joints,
  strong vital heart;
  each sense and organ,
  cell and nerve
  serving as it was meant
  to serve—
  free of hindrance,
  pain, or strife—
  the glad expressiveness
  of life.
In quiet periods of prayer
we feel the healing Presence near
assuring the receptive soul:
"I Am that life. Be thou made whole!"

A Patient Person

Dorothy Pierson

Dear God,
In becoming the patient person
I so long to be,
Let me exercise all the love I feel for You.
Within me there are deep knowings
Of Your constant love.
No matter how forgetful or ignorant
My growing self may be,
You hold me in Your sight
As Your beloved child.
Help me, God, to grow in patience
As I live my life with people,
Each no less Your child than I.
Let me remember to free others
That they may know of Your love too.
Help me to give them room to find You
On their own path,
Not shadowed by my willful self, but free.

This is what I long to be,
A patient person.

Make of My Life a Prayer

Pamela Yearsley

Is prayer the moment that I cease all outer things
And seek to become one with the essence of God?
Does it begin when I whisper "Dear Father"
And end with a reverent "Amen"?
Is it only there when I listen in stillness
For some wordless answer to mirror my thoughts?
I pray not.

Make of my life a prayer;
Of my waking and sleeping, breathing and talking,
Of my laughing and crying and running and walking;
Make of my life a prayer.

Let me not be left waiting for the praying of others,
For supplications or magic to perfect my way.
Let me eat and drink, move and think
On things of love nature.
Let it glow through my living
And loving and changing.
Make of my life a prayer.

Lord, Use Me

James Dillet Freeman

Lord, use me as I may be used.
Let what I have to give be given.
Let no one say, *He has refused;*
Let no one think, *He has not striven.*

Lord, use me—this is all I pray—
For your own purpose, great or small,
That by my being here I may
Contribute to the good of all.

Poetry of the
Seasons and Holidays

Spring Cleaning

Fred Millham

Mother Nature's busy now
  With cloth and mop and broom.
She's doing her spring cleaning
  To sweep out winter's gloom.
She's packing all the snowflakes
  And icicles away.
She's wrapping up the winter winds
  And gloomy skies of gray.
She's bringing out the boxes
  That hold the signs of spring—
A carton full of dewdrops
  And bubbling brooks that sing;
A barrel full of daffodils
  That bloom without a care,
And crates of lovely lilacs
  To perfume the warming air.
And from a very special trunk
  That opens with a glow,
Out comes the surest sign of spring—
A freshly washed rainbow.

Early Gardening

Katherine Hanley

Those first shoots are always a surprise.
What with the snow and all, I'd forgotten
Not how hardy they are
But how frail.
The meek inherit the Earth again.

Voice of the Crocus

Mildred N. Hoyer

Bedded in tranquillity,
Blanketed with silence,
I slept.
But now, while winter lingers,
Slowly, slowly,
There comes the nudge of life
That will not be denied,
 The urge to seek the light.
 Slowly, slowly, I find my way
 Through darkness of the soil,
 Upward, ever upward
  Until the final thrust
  That penetrates the dark
  To let the doubting see
  Resurrected life in me.

Belief

Winifred Heiskell Layton

I have known such lovely things,
walked with beauty many springs
that I have lived, then in my heart
when winter shrieks cacophonies,
dear April zephyr harmonies
heal with all their blending art.
Beneath the crystal crust
green things grow.
Before the world sees them
God tells me so.

Spring Snow

L. A. Davidson

The pear tree snowed last night
across the lawn. The drifts of white
showed clean and fresh at dawn.

Spring hung along the virgin bough
just yesterday. Night passed, and now
ripe summer holds brief sway.

In petals cast upon the grass
the promise grows. It will surpass
this transient form when summer goes.

Lost and Found

John D. Engle, Jr.

So gradually my golden girl withdrew
And so quietly I hardly knew
That she had gone away at all until
A dark cloud draped itself across the hill,
The dying grass curled up in livid pain,
And cold winds shook the dead leaves down like rain.

But today my golden girl returned.
I saw her dancing where the jonquils burned
Their yellow trail by the margin of a lake.
She was the same sweet child. I saw her wake
The sleeping trees and thaw out all the rills
As she bounced her sun ball through the hills.
She smiled at me, still full of fun and play—
Pretending she had never been away.

My Heart Makes Its Own Weather

James Dillet Freeman

My heart makes its own weather,
  So let the world grow gray;
My heart starts saying April
  When April's far away.

In spite of rain and reason
  And winter on the wing,
My heart has its own season,
  And my heart says it is spring!

Blow wind and bitter weather,
  Come care and whistling cold,
An April heart will never
  Grow gray or crabbed or old.

Time is a wrinkled treason;
  Age is an old untruth.
Heart, keep your changeless season,
  Green April, golden youth!

Morning of Light

Hal Lingerman

Never the same—
Now, forevermore, this Earth
Ablaze
in Christ's
Embrace
Of light.

Never again the same—
Mountains, trees, and streams
Shining
Easter morning
Lining
Hearts with light.

Nevermore the same—
Now our souls are quickened,
Alive
To love in Christ;
Alive
To hear within,
To give without,
To share the gift of life.

A Promise in March

Dorothy Pierson

O God,
I open myself as wide
As this sky and these fields
To Your holy presence.
As the new buds and blossoms hold promise
Of beauty and fragrance,
So Your presence in me
Holds promise of wondrous good.
I do not doubt in the face of the March sky.
Clouds pass and dissipate,
Patches of blue confirm that
The vault of heaven is untouched!

In the bleakness of any of life's experiences,
A deep assurance of eternity
Holds me steady and strong.
I draw on the resurrecting Christ within.
Just as the Earth draws on the power of life,
I draw on the seed of my own Christ image,
And through the power of God's perfection in me,
I spring forth into newness of life!

Like the Whisper of Spring

Sally R. Joy

As buds burst forth from gray branches,
   And green shoots poke through the sod,
So Easter comes gently into our lives,
   Like a whispered message from God.

Renewing our spirits, restoring our hopes,
   Revising our theories of how aims are achieved—
Easter contains a challenge for us
   To believe more than we yet have believed.

It is well that Easter should come in spring,
   In a season well-marked by fresh starts;
For sorrows and failures can be left behind
   When it's Easter in human hearts.

Picking Violets

Virginia Scott Miner

Yesterday I picked violets,
a great crystal bowl of them,
so there would be fewer ruined
today when I hung out clothes.

But when I took the basket
out into sun and breeze,
there, overnight, violets
had bloomed again,
winking among the grass.

Undiscouraged, undemanding,
beautiful . . .
love is like that.

Flower of May

R. H. Grenville

After the final frost, the wind and showers,
come the open smiles of Maytime flowers —
smooth as porcelain, shell-tinted, white,
and golden-hearted, they evoke delight.

But even as I gaze, in part, I see
tight, frosted buds upon a leafless tree;
amid bleak buffetings through winter hours,
only the small and secret *hope* of flowers.

So, often, when a blessing-joy unfolds
to thrill my being with its heart of gold,
I realize it did not come full-blown
from out of nowhere, but in faith was sown
in times of turbulence and winter gray —
a prayer-seed *knowing* it would bloom in May.

Summer Day

Pauline Havard

They say that it is senseless to pretend
There are no shadowy places in this world
Of ours; that we have only joy to spend,
And sunlight's banners always are unfurled.
But on a day like this I half-believe
The world is thus—a place of constant sun;
Green meadows where the heart forgets to grieve
And there are flowers and light for everyone.
On such a day as this, with sky a clear
Lapis-luzuli blue, without a cloud,
It would be sacrilege to shed a tear
Or voice complaints in a tone sharp and loud;
On days like this I feel each moment's fashioned
For giving thanks, unmeasured and unrationed.

Summer Rain

Jamie Autenrieth

As it falls from velvet clouds, I hear the laughter of the
    rain,
I feel the coolness kiss my check, and know God's love
    will never wane.
He soothes the sun-scarred Earth with drops becoming
    giant seas,
And washed away are dark, sad thoughts; refreshed and
    clean, the grass and trees.
Muffled wheels of thunder roll throughout hills and
    valleys, free.
They add a certain richness to the rain-choir's misty
    melody.
And lightning flings his abstract art across a cloud-laced
    pearly sky,
Reminding me that God is light, and darkness leaves us
    by and by.
Drop by drop, a thousand drummings, living heartbeat,
    life sustained;
A vibrant joy within me rises to the laughter of the rain.

The Seed Unto the Seed Returned

Frances Elliott

This is the ultra verdant time;
Green lushness topped with azure blue,
The fullness of the leaf and stem
And variety of floweret hue.

This is the ultra verdant time;
The fruit of mind, the food for soul
Now unite and form the rhyme
Of beauty, truth, and cosmic whole.

This is the ultra verdant time;
The journey made, the lesson learned,
Creator and created one,
The seed unto the seed returned.

Summer Postscript

John D. Engle, Jr.

Queen Anne has laced up
the August world
with wonder
while maturing corn,
born of beauty,
rustles a green symphony.
Tasseled and silked,
it dances with delight,
paired with an unseen partner.
Field-fringing trees
join in with joy
while all their leaves applaud
another summer blessing
sent from God.

Unseasonable

John D. Engle, Jr.

It's a delightful
April day.
The wind is warm;
the sky is blue,
except for herds
of cattle clouds
that now and then
come grazing through.

It is the kind
of April day
that I will
long remember—
for God delivered
it to me
in the middle
of November.

A Spring Day in the Fall

Clara Baldwin

How rich, how rare
A spring day in the fall!
A high clear blue
Sparkling on the fruiting world,
Yellows burnished into gold,
Reds a heady wine.
All nature spurred alive
For one final fling.
Leaves fall like golden rain,
Acorns rattle down,
Migrating birds hesitate,
　　an added flourish in their call.
Bees work these last fateful hours,
　　as an extra dividend,
A respite in a world too often filled with woe.
A gift to lift, a gift of hope
　　in nature's golden time.
A golden gift:
A bright fall day of spring!

Autumn Abundance

Harold Whaley

We give thanks, our Father-God,
For golden days of burnished radiance,
For lingering leaves that burst in flames
Of scarlet and crimson on stalwart oaks,
While chattering, scampering squirrels
Frisk among a riot of acorn abundance
Designed for their winter supply.
Wonder stirs our hearts
As we observe the divine pattern
Of wild geese in flight
Across a wind-blown autumn sky!
The sweet fragrance of ripened purple grapes
And wafts of pungent smoke
Evoke remembered loveliness.
Distant sheaves of harvest grain,
Fields of ripened corn and squash,
Fences of burnt orange bittersweet,
The trailing russet vines—
All yield a rush of enchantment that excites
Continued praise for luxuriant providence.
For all Thy magnitude of love expressed,
We bring grateful hearts in thankfulness!

September

Martha Smock

There is no perceptible change,
Yet change is in the air.
I feel it, I sense it, I welcome it.
Like a September day,
Which can still feel like summer
Or can already seem like fall,
So my heart has its ninth month,
When what has been wants to linger,
And what is to come wants to enter.
It is a time when change is imminent,
A time for long-held dreams to flower,
A time for the growing season,
Which sometimes seemed so long a time,
To make way for full fruition.

October

Martha Smock

October days are days
When time stands still.
The air seems breathless now
With expectation.
A lone bird sings;
Leaves flutter and fall
In golden showers;
And, hovering over all—
A sense of God's abiding,
Shining love.

Field

John D. Engle, Jr.

This field of snow
this moment
holds for me
just as much
of God's divinity
as it will hold
when springtime
warms the hours
and makes this field of snow
a field of flowers.
For I have learned that God
has endless ways
of making known
the beauty He portrays.
This field, indeed,
is but an instrument
on which God plays
inspired and eloquent
variations touching every heart
that is responsive
to each season's art.
Winter, springtime, summertime, and fall
echo the master theme: His love for all.

Early Rising

Winifred Brand

Rise before the dawn tomorrow,
though the air be bleak and chill.
Let the day come on you softly,
pausing on your windowsill.
Watch the changing shadows lighten . . .
skies turn gently, softly gray.
Listen, through the predawn darkness
how trusting songsters greet the day.
Watch the dawn's light grow and deepen,
though winter still may hide the sun . . .
In your heart you'll feel the blessing,
God's greatest gift . . . Today . . . has come!

Softly, White and Pure

Dorothy R. Fulton

In stillness, I wait.
Within the calm lies the
expectant tension that is
prelude to a snowfall;
Then, softly, white and pure,
peace settles on my soul
erasing imperfections,
uniting me with others
like a snow blanket blotting out
boundaries until
road and tree and house are one.

Thanks Giving

Verle Bell

My heart spills over with gratitude.
Joy wells out of me for life . . .
my life . . . my specialness.
For there is no one else
in this whole world
or in all the worlds
like me.
I am.
I.
I have always been.
I shall always be.
In humility and awe, I give thanks.

What have I realized,
from eons of conscious existence?
I have learned sometimes to stumble
rather than to plunge headlong
where I ought not to go . . .
To fall and pick myself up,
righted and rebalanced so that
I can find new direction.
Shrubs are there to clutch when needed
to keep me from falling down the cliff
when my feet have slipped.

I have learned, too, to give a hand
to other travelers on the trail
when they falter or grow weary.
And I am learning to leave them
if they want to go another way
or at a different pace.

I have learned to keep my eyes
trained more surely on the glow
at the top of the Holy Mountain,
paying less heed to the sideward nooks.
But if I lose my direction at a crossing
and wander off the Way
I have learned to turn around
and retrace my steps,
instead of following to its end.

Most of all, Father, I have learned that
I am Your beloved child.

My own headstrong will has never brought me
peace.
Peace comes,
along with deep, high gratitude
and joy,
only when I think Your thoughts
and will Your will.

So it is,
And so shall it ever be.

Song of Thanksgiving

Jean S. Platt

For cardinals in the wintertime
and robins in the spring,
For mourning doves the year around,
be glad, my heart, and sing!
For holly in December
and trillium in May,
for daisies blooming wild and free
upon a summer's day;
For Christmas joy and New Year's hope,
the promise Easter brings:
for all life's blessings, large and small,
my heart, enraptured, sings.

Quiescent

R. H. Grenville

There is a strength in calm,
in quietness,
that active energies
do not possess.
A waiting calm,
the calm of quiet knowing,
precedes all impetus
of vital growing,
a fact I rediscover as I go
past patient trees in a landscape
under snow.

140

The Shepherds

Anita Wheatcroft

First came the shepherds.
   The childlike always come to Him
   More quickly, regardless of their age.
Wise men deliberate, weigh costs,
And plan. They buy elaborate gifts,
   Then wait, till stars and signs are right.
   But shepherds, trusting,
   Travel light.
Only themselves they bring.

The Miracle of Christmas

Martha Smock

Not Herod in his palace,
   Not mighty men or strong,
But simple shepherds keeping watch
   First heard the angels' song.

Their names are not remembered,
   Who knows their lives or ways?
We only know that heavenly hosts
   Sang them their songs of praise.

The miracle of Christmas
   Had its beginning when
God sent His greatest message
   To ordinary men.

The Christmas Harp

William Trall Doncaster, Jr.

Blithe music from a Christmas harp
Strung with a thousand strings
Sent echoes through the centuries
With sounds of higher things.

Its music swelled in Bethlehem,
Crescendoed when a birth
Behind a worn old stable door
Would chance to change the earth.

As from some deep, unfailing source
The wonder of that song!
A harp that holds a thousand strings
Could keep its tune so long.

A Christmas Window

Elizabeth Searle Lamb

Caught there in the stained glass:
   Madonna and Child
      how the light
streaming through leaded panes
breaks into rainbows
about her head
      how His face
becomes more than a child's face

      and how the rays
beaming from His hands are healing rays
   Madonna and Child
and how the light flowing through
is more than light, is indeed
more Light than light
      more Faith than faith
and more even than love
      is Love.

143

My Christmas Wish

Grace E. Gimbel

I made my Christmas wish tonight
mid flickering candles and carols sung.
I wished for the vision to see the light
through the eager eyes of the very young.
I wished for their hope which no force defies
as they wait for the day of the Holy Birth.
For the trust and belief in every child's eyes,
I wished for joy and peace on Earth.

My Christmas wish was answered tonight
mid flickering candles and carols sung.
I felt the power of the light
as I stood and watched with the very young.
Each star was a promise from skies above,
each shadow a hovering angel's wing.
Through the eyes of a child, I learned it is love
that reflects the light of the newborn King.

Christ Is Born

Verle Bell

The instant dawn's first tinge is seen,
  Promise of a new day is at hand.
Before the eye can discern a break in darkness,
  Birds are cheerfully declaring,
  "Morning is coming!"
Before this prophecy can be disputed,
  Streaks of rose and gold paint the sky,
And roosters on the ground
  And larks on high are shouting:
    "Morning is here!"

The moment hope comes to a doubting heart,
  The promise of the Christ is made.
Who can explain this lift in the spirits?
  No logic can account for it,
  But it is there . . .
No question about it, life is brighter!
  The song in the heart has changed
From minor to major, from sad to glad.
  The overwhelming surge of joy declares:
    Christ is born!

On Christmas Eve

R. H. Grenville

Snow that falls on Christmas Eve
is lovelier than other snow,
and has a greater gentleness,
almost as though
it were a fleece that angels spun
to swaddle Mary's newborn Son.

Stars that shine on Christmas Eve
are brighter than all other stars.
It is as though Love looks through them,
beholding mankind's many scars,
and signals, "Do not be forlorn.
To you, this night, a Child is born."

The songs we sing on Christmas Eve,
how beautiful they are, and dear!
The link the present with the past
and bring the holy angels near.
Like joyous pilgrims, led by them,
our hearts arrive in Bethlehem.

Your Christmas Guest

James Dillet Freeman

Take time this Christmas Day to go
  A little way apart
And with the hands of prayer prepare
  The house that is your heart.

Brush out the dusty fears, brush out
  The cobwebs of your care
Till in the house that is your heart
  It's Christmas everywhere.

Light every window up with love,
  And let your love shine through,
That they who walk outside may share
  The blessed light with you.

Then will the rooms with joy be bright,
  With peace the hearth be blessed,
And Christ Himself will enter in
  To be your Christmas guest.

Birth—Awareness

Laurie Killam

The whisper of wings—
The crisp feel of straw beneath
   my soft new body—
Do I hear the tinkle of little bells
That encircle the neck of that beast,
   and the bleating of a little lamb?
What adoration in the beautiful
   countenance gazing down at me,
While the arm encased in coarse
   linen embraces me yet so tenderly!
Is that the glitter of princely raiment
   rustling in the shadows?
Do I smell the fragrance of incense and
   spices—pungent and so familiar?
In awe and wonder I catch glimpses
Of a dark blue canopy far above me
   studded with a host of twinkling lights!
And the taste of fresh night air as it brushes
   my lips and caresses my cheek so softly.
The question forms, and lingers, hovering
   over the precious tableau—
Will I fill the world with love?
It is all so right and perfect—
     I am here.

Christmas Within an Inner Silence

Elizabeth Searle Lamb

Beyond celebration
of gift and carol,
candlelighting and
"Merry Christmas!"
there is another
ritual of season
when I turn within
to the still center
of my own being,
celebrating
within the shape
of silence
the star radiance
the birth love
the peace angel
and let vibrations
flow out from
that center's energy
to bless, to heal,
to give the gift
of radiant love.

Mary Speaks

Neville Braybrooke

A stable was the last place I would have chosen.
When Joseph and I set out for the census in Jerusalem,
We had no idea that my time was so close.
Perhaps the long ride by donkey hastened it.
I remember the doves circling round the Temple as we
     came through the city—
How softly their wings had fanned the air.

Bethlehem seemed like the end of the Earth;
It was full of people and there was nowhere to stay.
Exhausted, I sat in a courtyard while Joseph went off to
     make some arrangements.
I thought of Moses in the desert
And how, when he breathed upon the bitter wells, he
     sweetened them.
May the coming of my Child so change the world.

At last Joseph returned with an innkeeper who gave us
    shelter of a sort.
The hay was clean, and we could hear the slow, even
    breath of the oxen.
Then quite suddenly I knew for certain there would be no
    rest for me.
We had brought nothing for a birth,
And Joseph went running to the inn to fetch swaddling
    bands and help.
*May the borrowed clothes offered to my Child bandage
    the wounds of humanity.*

Now it is nearly morning and the sky is streaked with
    blue and gold—
Blue is the color of my mantle.
Joseph is kneeling beside me with my hand clasped
    between his.
It cannot be much longer I think before I shall hold the
    Child in my arms.
I have just said to Joseph, who must be nearly as tired as
    I am,
"Do you realize that you and I will be teaching the Son of
    God to walk?"

Joseph Speaks

Neville Braybrooke

I am tired of being thought of as an old man,
Leaning upon a staff.
My beard is not gray.
Many miles did I pace the stable floor on the night of the
      birth,
And many more did I walk beside the ass, bearing the
      mother and child,
On our flight into Egypt.

Yet when poets and painters came to tell my story, they
      altered the facts.
The painters gave my shoulders a stoop.
And the poets shortened my stride to a shuffle.
They were mistaken.
They confused age with authority.

My passions were those of any young Jew of my tribe,
My senses as keen.

From my bench I watched the shadow of my espoused
　　　grow fuller.
Had I been deceived—and by whom?
Other women when found out had been stoned to death
　　　by the people.
But at night in dreams I heard voices promising to make
　　　perfect the impossible.
Sometimes the villagers spoke of two-headed goats
And of calves deformed at birth.
I said nothing.
I thought of the mysterious conception in my *own house*.
Was I mistaken when I heard the beating of wings?
(There were nests in the trees nearby.)
Words formed in my mind and became a consolation:
　　　"Fear not, Joseph."
Where did they spring from?
For beware—pride in the heart can nourish the
　　　imagination.
So I said to my soul: "Be patient, be still."

The wings and the voices persisted:
My confidence grew in the Word.

The House of David would have a new Lord.

The Inn-Keeper's Wife

Joy Anne Quay

"O go on out, Elizabeth," she said.
"You may as well go out and watch the star.
A modest Jewish maiden does not show
Her face in such a godless place as this.
You've done your chores? O that I doubt!
You're dreamy-eyed, and pay but scant attention
To the duties which a maid must learn
Before she marries. But you'll learn in time,
I'll wager, if Jehovah—bless His holy name—
Should send a man to be a husband to you.
Although you have no beauty that a man
Should look on you with favor. Yet some man,
Old and devout, may need a maiden but to serve
His needs. Like the one who came tonight
With his young wife. They're in the stable now.
And she with child. What more could I do?
There is no place for them in here. I do
The best I can. Life's not an easy lot,
I'll tell you that. You wait until you're thirty,
As I am, and you have borne six children;

154

And wrinkles twist around your lovely eyes;
And your hair is dull—why mine is almost gray!   ,
And your hands—you see these hands of mine?
So rough and cracked, I hide them when I can
Beneath this apron. Once the young men called
My hands as beautiful as Esther's or as Ruth's.
But now I scour these floors with lye, and so
They're almost burned away. O do not cry,
You foolish child! I only tell you this
About my hands to make you see the Star
Means nothing!
              O very well. I'll look at it."

She stood with Elizabeth and watched the Star.
The night seemed full of some great unknown Presence.
A quiet splendor filled the air, and tears
That she had held too long inside ran down
Her tired cheeks, and she held Elizabeth.
Then from the stable came an ageless sound.
"The baby's born!" she cried, and felt the thrill
Of something beautiful, almost forgotten:
        "For unto us a Child is born;
          Unto us a Son is given."
And holding her daughter close against the cold,
She hurried toward the stable and the Babe.

Like a Mighty Tide

Wilferd A. Peterson

Christmas is not in tinsel, lights and outward show;
The secret lies in an inner glow.
It's lighting a fire inside the heart,
Good will and joy are a vital part.
It's a higher thought and a greater plan,
It's a glorious dream in the soul of man,
Christmas begins deep down inside,
Then engulfs the world like a mighty tide.

Nativity

Winifred Brand

I thank thee, Lord,
that in the manger
of my heart
lies infant love
to grow in wisdom . . .
to wax strong . . . and come at length
into its full expression,
the Christ in me.

The New Year

Mary Carolyn Davies

As young as you,
   As young as I,
Waits the New Year!
   So let us try
As we grow, together, we
Fortunate and happy three,
To be as kind as we can be,
As full of joy and bravery,
As understanding and as gay
As we may, each speeding day.
Let us keep the year as white
As it is this New Year's night,
As stainless and as shining, till
The year grows old, as young years will.
While the world is kneeling now
Shaping brave its new-year vow
Let us make a vow, and, more,
Keep our vow as ne'er before,
This year we will strive to give
Service, kindness, joy, to live
Less for self, and more for all.
We will listen to the call
Of duty, and of beauty too.
We'll do the tasks we're loath to do,
We'll smile when we would like to frown,
Lift ourselves up when we feel down;
We'll seek to give, not always take;
We'll seek to build, not always break.
And, day on day, we'll make this year
A sure foundation, and we'll rear
Upon it, building strong and well,
The future, our firm citadel.

All New

Mildred N. Hoyer

It is the newness
Of the New Year—
Like that of a new home
Waiting to be lived in,
Filled with promise.

It is the newness,
The new beginning,
The letting go
Of all that is past
And moving forward,
Ever forward,
Into unfolding newness,
Ever forward
Toward fulfillment.

The Light Touch

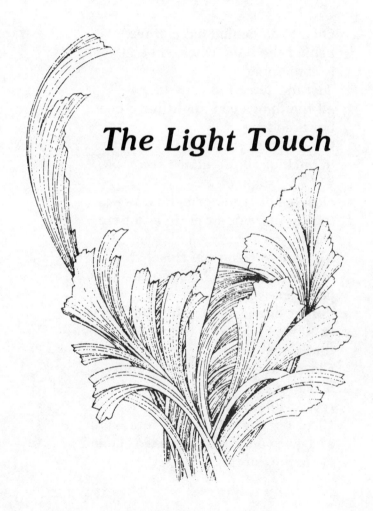

On the Shelf

Mark Magruder

On a shelf behind old clothes,
behind the hats, where no one goes,
is something.
Just the same today as then —
all the things you might have been,
but aren't.
Oh, it's true you've got to look
in back of all the things you took,
      then left . . .
closets full of things behind
that bother you from time to time.
But look,
it's time to clean the closet shelf
and be content to be yourself—
you *are!*
Forget the one you might have been
(way back, you don't remember when)—
that's gone.
Closets filled with stuff like that
leave no room for your new hat;
rest awhile.
Clear out the things that lurk behind
and give yourself some peace of mind . . .
close the door!

Waspies, Bees, and Alligators

Leonard J. Kovar

Browsing through some old papers, I stumbled across this little bedtime prayer spoken by one of my children at age five and a half. It had so impressed me that I had written it down verbatim:

> Thank You, God, for a nice day.
>   And I love my family,
> And I love everyone in the whole world,
> And I love everyone in the whole world,
>   And every things . . .
> But there are lots of things I don't know;
>   I don't know lots of things . . .
> But I know butterflies,
> And I know waspies,
> And I know bees,
> And I know alligators.
>   Amen.

Well, I don't know everything either. In fact, I am not sure that I know butterflies, waspies, or alligators; but I do know this, that in the innocence of childhood, that little person knew what was important: life, love, and the wonder of growth.

> The cure for the pessimist lies
>   in good deeds.
> Who toils for another forgets
>   his own needs.
>   —*Ella Wheeler Wilcox*

The Rainbow

Frances Elliott

The Earth is smiling through its tears;
And now in colors soft array
Across the meadow there appears
A rainbow, bowing down to pray.

A Pleasant Surprise

Willa R. Jackson

What a pleasant surprise God is to me.
I should take Him for granted by now,
        you see,
but He never stops amazing me.
What a pleasant surprise He continues
        to be!

Suppose

Betty Miller

Suppose the seed
        set into the soil to
        burst open,
        sprout out,
        reach skyward,
Saw only darkness as
        Truth.

Bridges

Virginia Scott Miner

Bridges are ecumenical things—
bonds, not barriers,
joinings, not separations—
for each side says
to its brother,
"I'll come halfway
from my side to yours
if you'll do the same
from the other."

Beautiful Accident

John D. Engle, Jr.

Brooms of breezes
swept the clouds away,
leaving the floor of heaven
clean and blue
to tidy up
the ending
of the day.
And then sleepy Evening
stumbled through
the colored lane that led
to Twilight's door,
spilling a billion diamonds
on the floor.

Exercise

J. Sig Paulson

Here's the best exercise
   you'll ever find:
Simply think the thoughts
   that s-t-r-e-t-c-h your mind.

Spending a Day

Mary Carolyn Davies

Splendid things may happen!
Oh, of course they may;
But thinking of tomorrow
Is no way to spend today!

Windows

Winifred Heiskell Layton

I pray that I'm a window
for the sun to sparkle through
even if others prefer
art glass of brilliant hue.
I would have God's love
shine through me
so everyone will say:
"I didn't even see the glass,
but what a lovely day!"

For and About Children

Blessing for a Child

Jim Rosemergy

Blessed be this child of God
  whose very beginning is as our own.
May he feel his kinship with the Spirit of the universe
  and his brotherhood with all mankind.

Blessed be this child of love
  who reflects the love of God for man.
May he feel the love others give to him, the love he gives
      to others,
    and come to know there is but one love . . . God.

Blessed be this child of life
  whose very being stems from the action of God.
May life always flow easily within him,
    and may he increase the movement of God within
      others.

Blessed be this child of wisdom
  whose ever-expanding mind will touch the fount of
      knowing.
May he learn to listen to the words and feelings of
      others,
    and to the voice of God in prayer, for through these
      come understanding.

Blessed be this child of eternity
  who has no Alpha and no Omega.
May the path he walks always lead him to the highest
  pinnacles of life, love, and wisdom,
And may he guide others by the life he lives.

Thank You, Father, for another expression of Your
  eternal, loving presence.

Individuality

Henrietta Liebknecht

As each grain of shifting sand
  Upon the shore of sea,
Each flake of snow shows forth
  Its perfect form of symmetry,
So each child bears the stamp of
  His very own Divinity.

Dream On My Soul

Hettie Wallace

Dream on my soul,
Though dreaming has outgrown
The shining raiment
Childhood's dreams had worn.
They still can be as fair,
And still as true,
As those that blessed you
And each day anew.
It matters not
Just when or where or why
The Glory waned—
It is enough to cry,
"Father once more
Make me a little child,
Give me glad dreams again,
Let me be reconciled
To earlier faith,
To love that feels no fear,
To joy that ever knows
Thou art with me here.

I Found a Little Tree

Opal Dean Young

Last spring I found a little tree
As sad as it could be.
A big tree's branches shaded it,
And no sun could it see.

I dug it up so tenderly—
Its roots all caked with dirt—
And took it to a sunny spot
And dug down through the turf.

I stood the little tree up straight,
Covered its roots with rich, moist sod,
Tamped the ground firmly all around,
And left the rest to God.

Now a new spring has come today,
And my dear little tree
Spreads its branches far and wide,
The size of nearly three!

Oh, thank You, God, for love and care
Of little trees and me.

To a Child Just Awakened

John D. Engle, Jr.

What strange lands
have you been traveling
that leave such dreams
still glowing in your eyes?
What secret songs
of beauty would you sing
if tongue and memory
could harmonize?
Yours is the calming face
of relaxation,
sculptured by sleep.
Your eyes reflect the far
and sacred mountains
of imagination
from which you have
not quite returned.
You are all dressed now,
but your usual chatter
sleeps in the quiet
enigma of your face.
Your thoughts seem busy
with some wordless matter
that you have borrowed
from nocturnal space.
No doubt, this grown-up world
seems rather odd
to you, a child
who spent the night with God.

The Little Wise Ones

Carleen S. Hamilton

The wise ones
  dream a million things,
Like yellow suns
  that walk on springs
    and light the world.

The wise ones
  know important things,
Like where to look
  for tinted wings
    and watch them fly.

The wise ones
  hear with burning minds
The music
  that we've left behind
    and lost somehow.

The wise ones
  listen while we teach,
Yet higher
  than a man can reach
    they touch and grasp.

Questions

Lillian K. Webb

I saw a honeybee in a flower;
Seemed like I watched him half an hour.
Flitting and buzzing—now isn't it funny?
A little old bee knows how to make honey!

I watched some birds way up in a tree
Making a nest; I was still as could be.
Then I tried to make one. I tried so hard!
But mine fell apart; now isn't that odd?

Our baby duckling, yellow and soft,
Ran to the pond and paddled off.
But I don't even know how to swim!
Who in the world do you guess taught him?

How can they do these things? They're so small,
You wouldn't think they had sense at all!
Instinct? What's that? Oh, I think I know—
It's God thinking for them—He loves them so!

Reach Out

Sharon M. Behr

I recall the words my mother said when I was very small,
And so afraid to reach out for fear that I might fall:
"You must have faith to walk, my child, before you can
      go far,
"But with that faith you'll find the way to reach your
      brightest star."
Then believing is the key for what you want to be,
Seeing not with eyes alone, but seeing inwardly.
For what if the little bird that's hatching feared to come
      out and sing?
He'd never know the beautiful Truth that he was born to
      take wing.
Reach out, believe, be not afraid, but take a giant stride.
How joyous is the knowledge that God is by your side!

Where Is Love?

Dee Lillegard

Love is where you find it.
You only have to look.
It's in the birds and butterflies
And down along the brook.

Love is on the mountain.
Love is in the sky.
Love is in the earth below
And in the clouds up high.

God has placed love everywhere
(though it's not on maps or charts).
Best of all, He sent His love
To fill our minds and hearts.

Why a Turtle Smiles

Lola Sneyd

A turtle can carry
　　His house on his back,
And rain won't come in
　　Because there's no crack.

He's snug and secure,
　　For he's waterproof!
No wonder he smiles
　　At rain on his roof.

Twelve Friends

Dee Lillegard

January gently opens the door.
February takes a peek.
March blows it open a little more.
April starts to speak.
She chirps to May, "What have we here?"
June says, "Only half a year."
July decides to open wide.
August boldly steps inside.
September follows, dressed in gold.
October says, "We're getting old."
November replies, "Be of good cheer.
Merry days will soon be here."
December comes, then shuts the door.
Of what they do, I can say no more.
The twelve of them are now complete,
And here's *another* year to greet!

The Quizzical Rabbit

Ruth Stewart Schenley

A bunny has such
An asking nose;
His upper lip makes questions
Everywhere he goes.

He keeps discussing with himself
His endless wants and fears,
For all the things his nose asks,
He answers with his ears.

175

The Real Me

Linda L. Rogers

I've never raced in outer space,
But I'd love to be the first
To raise a sail on a comet's tail
And tour the universe!

    I've never fed banana bread
    To a boa in a baobab tree,
    But I don't need a daring deed
    To prove myself to me!

  It's the real me that I've gotta be.
  I want you to see; it's the real me!

I wear as many faces
As a crowd of circus clowns.
Sometimes I pin a green-bean grin
Upon a frumpy frown.

    But if I place another face
    On the one that's really mine,
    The "me" I hid that's down inside
    No one will ever find!

  It's the real me that I've gotta be.
  I want you to see; it's the real me!

A boa and me in a baobab tree
Are really only dreams,
And setting sail on a comet's tail
May not be what it seems.

I might not race in outer space
But I'll be satisfied
To dance to the beat of my own feet
And walk the world with pride!

It's the real me that I've gotta be.
I want you to see; it's the real me!

God Is Here

Rosemary Torrez

I see God
In the morning's colored sky,
In the birds with wings to fly,
In the children passing by.

I feel God
In the sun so warm on me,
In the shade beneath a tree,
In the puppy on my knee.

I hear God
In the wind that blows at night,
In the snowfall soft and white,
And in my thoughts so true and right.

A Game Called First

Evelyn Smith

Today I'll play a game called FIRST.
I made it up myself.
It isn't just some kind of game
You take down from a shelf.

Today I'll count how many times
That I'm the very first
To be my best in all I do—
Not ending up the worst.

Today I'm going to be the first
To say, "Good morning, everyone!"
And then I'll try to be the first
To get my chores all done.

Today I'll be the first to smile,
Without even keeping track
Of whomever I may smile at
Who doesn't smile right back.

Today why don't you be the first
To play this game with me?
Tomorrow, maybe, the whole wide world—
What a nice first that would be!

The Answer

Harlene Raban

Look around you and applaud:
The life you see all comes from God.

Daffodils and bearded goats,
Grizzly bears in furry coats,

All the world's creatures great or small,
If it weren't for God, wouldn't be here at all.

God walks through the wind
That makes the trees bend.

He colors the birds for their protection;
Butterflies hatch at His direction.

God is gravity that keeps us in place
As our world goes spinning around in space.

God is the smile on a dear one's face
And the love you feel in a warm embrace.

God is the invisible reason
Behind each day, behind each season.

When you see life and love, applaud—
You have just seen a part of God.

A Gift for Mother

Dee Lillegard

What shall I give to Mother,
Who gives so much to me?
A bright bouquet of flowers?
A young and growing tree?

A book, a bird, a bracelet,
Fancy paper and a pen—
I think I've found her just the thing.
I *think* I have. But then—

What shall I give, I wonder,
That can't be made or bought?
Something extra special,
Full of extra special thought.

I'll give her what she gives to me—
A smile, a helping way.
I'll give it not just once a year,
But every single day!

Thinking of Dad

Bette Killion

I like to think about the things
   my dad does every day,
How I watch him early mornings
   as he shaves his beard away,
How he kisses Mom and me good-bye,
   then with a smile and nod,
He starts the car, backs out our drive,
   and whirls off to his job.
Sometimes I watch him mow the lawn;
   sometimes we take a walk.
I like the way his eyebrows move
   as he listens to me talk.
But what I like to think about
   the most especially
Is when my dad, long, long ago,
   was just a boy like me.

Try

Margaret Finefrock

What in the world would our life be like
If no one ever tried?
What if Columbus let others convince him
He would fall off the other side?

Where would we be if the Wright Brothers
Decided man couldn't fly?
Or if Thomas Edison just gave up
And thought his goals too high?

What kind of life if Martin Luther King
Had not kept on with courage?
What if Eleanor Roosevelt had quit
The first time she became discouraged?

What kind of life can I create for myself
If I never even try?
Everything is possible if I know
My abundant Source of supply.

The strength to try is my very first step.
I know I can do and be
All things necessary for my highest good
Through the Presence of God in me.

INDEX

184

Printed U.S.A.   166-F-6589-20M-2-84